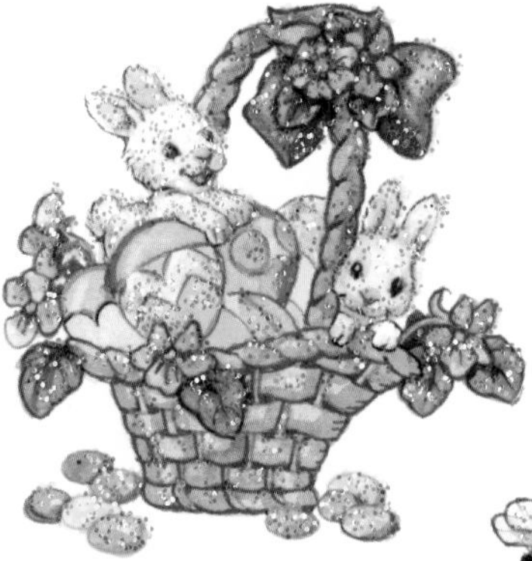
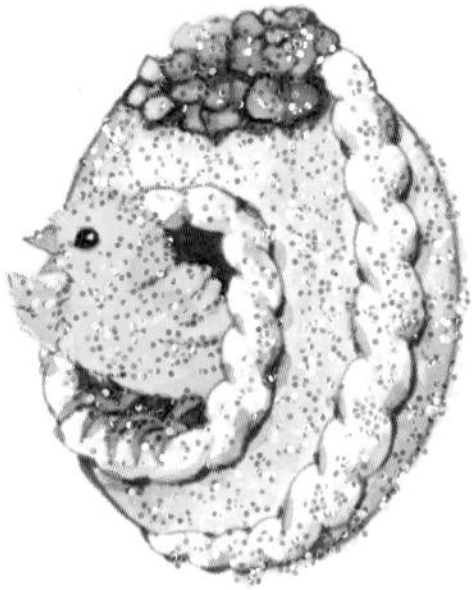
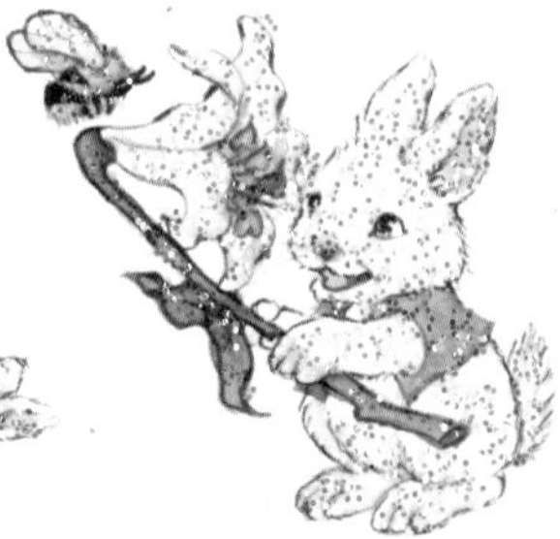
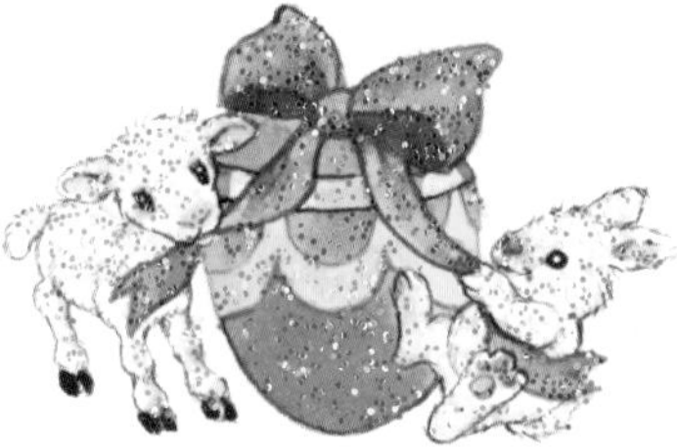
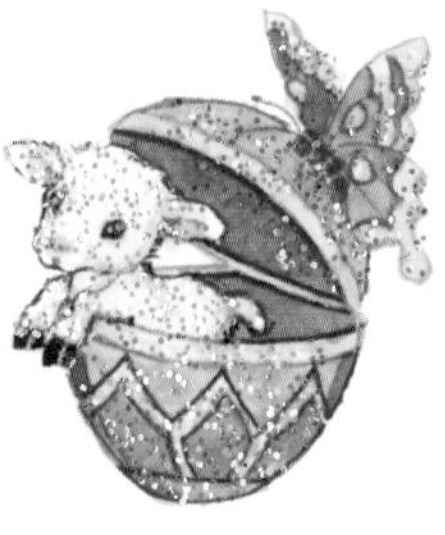
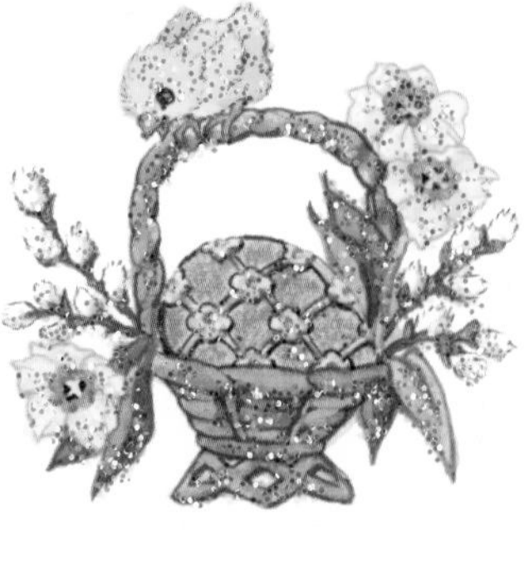

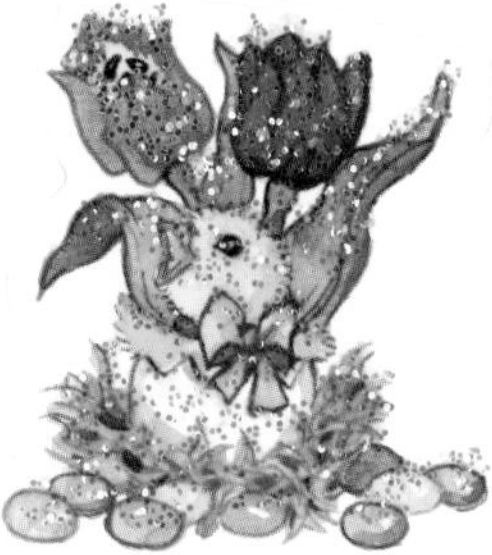

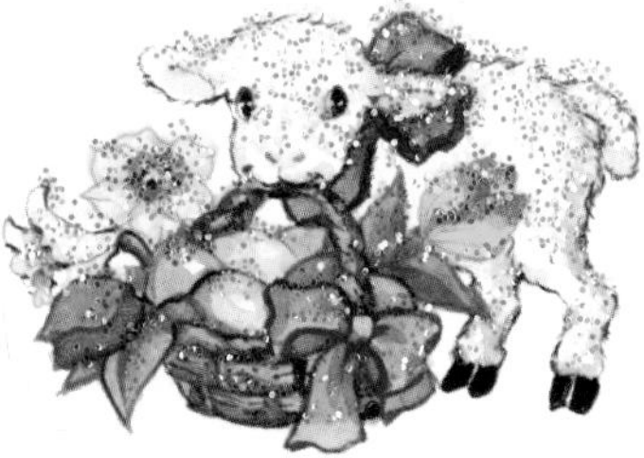

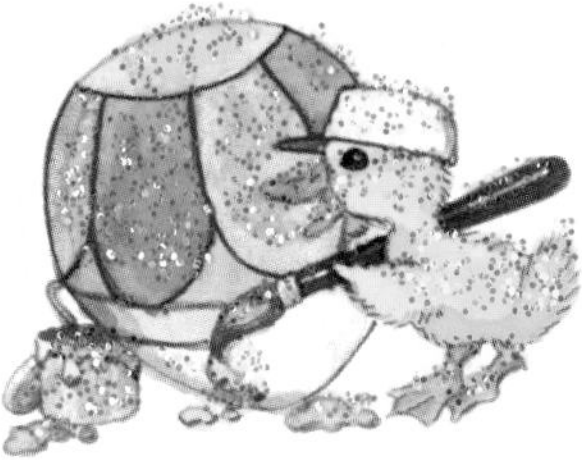

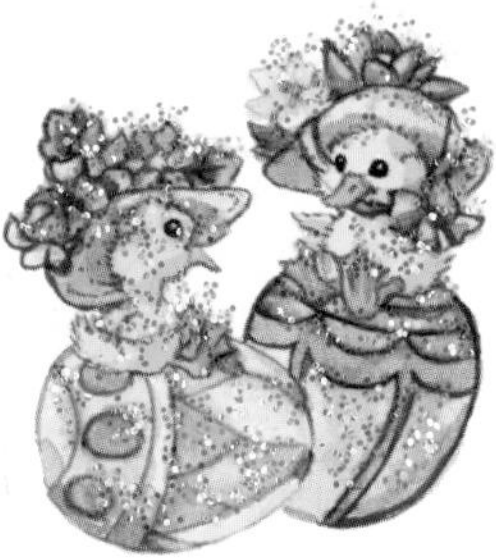

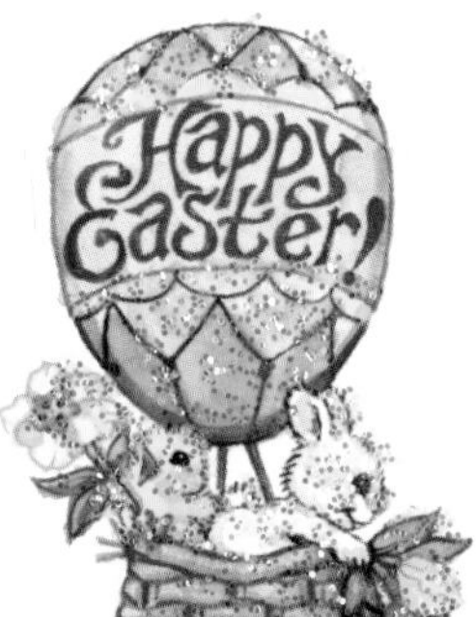
Happy Easter!

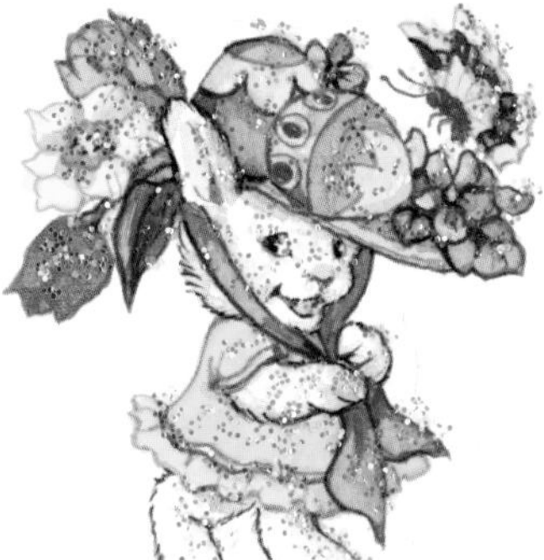